Glossary of Objectivist Definitions

by Ayn Rand

with additional entries by
Leonard Peikoff and Harry Binswanger

Edited by
Allison T. Kunze and Jean F. Moroney

AYN RAND
INSTITUTE PRESS

Published by
The Ayn Rand® Institute Press
aynrand.org

ISBN 978-0-9960101-8-4

TABLE OF CONTENTS

PREFACE

*The truth or falsehood of all
man's conclusions, inferences, thought and knowledge
rests on the truth or falsehood of his definitions.*
—Ayn Rand

Ayn Rand taught the importance of knowing exact definitions. In the course of her re-conceptualization of key philosophic issues, she formulated brilliant new definitions of many concepts. Building on her base, Leonard Peikoff has nearly doubled the number of philosophic terms formally defined by Objectivists.

This glossary was originally conceived as a compilation of these formal definitions. After reviewing the literature, however, we decided to broaden its scope to include terms that meet at least two of the following three criteria: (1) the term has a formal definition (or near to it); (2) it is philosophically important; (3) its meaning is dramatically clarified by Objectivism.

Thus, in addition to formal definitions, this glossary includes characterizations that are near-definitions of terms (though not meeting the requirements of formal definitions), statements of philosophic principles, and descriptions of axiomatic concepts. (Since axiomatic concepts can be defined only ostensively, the entries for these terms are merely descriptions.)

Often we had to choose between two or more similar statements for a single concept. In each case we tried to select the formulation that was the most complete and concise. We also preferred written formulations to oral ones.

Entries taken from oral presentations are marked "extemporaneous, unedited formulation," unless edited by the author himself. Although we took the wording from a literal transcript of the presentation, you should assume the formulation does not have the exactness of a written version. Note that this qualification applies to Ayn Rand's comments in the Appendix to *ITOE* (which she did not edit), but not to Leonard Peikoff's statements from his lecture course "The Philosophy of Objectivism" (as these were edited by him for inclusion in *The Ayn Rand Lexicon*).

Our primary concern in excerpting material was to avoid changing the meaning of the original. Thus, we have purposely kept excerpts long rather than edit them to make more concise statements. We have also preserved the phrase "in this context" from the original—we did not attempt to summarize the context in an editorial comment. Where we have added substantive words in brackets, these words were taken from the immediate surrounding context of the excerpted text. Exceptions and unusual excerpting are noted in the entry's reference.

In all cases, we encourage you to read the original sources and judge for yourselves whether or not these statements are indeed definitional, and in what context.

In each entry we have given the author and the reference for the quotation. In addition, if Ayn Rand's definition is quoted in *OPAR*, we include a reference to that discussion. For more cross-references, see the *Lexicon,* which has longer passages on more topics with extensive cross-referencing.

Unfortunately, the page numbering varies significantly among different editions of the books. As a result, you will notice some discrepancies between our page numbers and those in the *Lexicon* references and *OPAR* footnotes. The page numbers in our references refer to the *current paperback editions* of books, and to bound volumes of periodicals, as given in the source list. The chapter or article title is also included, in order to help readers with different editions find the quotation.

We have tried to minimize punctuation marks. Thus, all material in each entry is a direct quotation unless it appears in square brackets. Furthermore, we have omitted leading and trailing ellipses. The reader is alerted that many excerpts start or end mid-sentence. Again, we encourage you to look at the original.

In general, we have matched the formatting of the original. However, we used boldface type to highlight the term in each entry; if another means of highlighting the term was used in the original (e.g., italics), we omitted that formatting. When the entire definition was italicized or set off in parentheses, we omitted the italics or parentheses.

In the left-hand column, we have put some terms in quotation marks—those with informal names (e.g., "crow epistemology"), and those for invalid concepts (e.g., "duty"). However, in the body of the entry (the right-hand column) we have matched the quotation marks of the original.

Throughout the project, we were privileged to have the advice of Harry Binswanger. We would like to thank him for his invaluable help, and also for editing several of his own definitions for inclusion here.

We hope that you will find this a helpful resource, but in closing we would like to remind you of Dr. Peikoff's injunctions against the rationalistic misuse of definitions. (See his lecture course "Understanding Objectivism.") Definitions are a tool for directing your mind to reality; they are not a substitute for reality. A concept should stand in your mind, not as a string of words, but as an integration of concretes.

Ayn Rand was the first to grasp the objective nature of concepts, and therefore of the psycho-epistemological need for definitions. As she said,

> The purpose of a definition is to distinguish a concept from all other concepts and thus to keep its units differentiated from all other existents. . . . It enables man, not only to identify and *retain* a concept, but also to establish the relationships, the hierarchy, the *integration* of all his concepts and thus the integration of his knowledge. (*ITOE*, 40.)

She grasped this seminal truth and left behind a magnificent legacy of precise, illuminating definitions. Use them for what they are: signposts pointing to reality.

Jean F. Moroney
Allison T. Kunze
October, 1999

TO THE READER

I have authorized the use of Ayn Rand's and my own definitions in this work, but I have not read the manuscript. I cannot, therefore, vouch for the accuracy of any item; i.e., whether it is in fact, as herein claimed, either a definition or an essential principle of Objectivism. I suggest that, if in doubt, you go back to the original sources, and judge for yourself.

Let me reiterate here that only the material approved by Ayn Rand during her lifetime is part of Objectivism. Later definitions by me and Harry Binswanger are statements by knowledgeable Objectivists, but not therefore part of Objectivism.

I hope that this glossary will be a valuable reference tool for you in your future philosophical thinking.

Leonard Peikoff
Irvine, California
September 20, 1999

SOURCES

Below is reference information for the sources cited in the glossary. Please note that the page references in the glossary entries refer to the specific *paperback* editions, pamphlets, and bound periodicals listed here. These are the versions that are in print in 1999. We have included the following additional information in parentheses:

- Books: original publication information for the first edition of this book
- Pamphlets: reference for the original article
- Lectures: year recorded

By Ayn Rand

The Ayn Rand Column, Revised Second Edition. Edited by Peter Schwartz. Gaylordsville, CT: Second Renaissance Books, 1998. (First Edition: Oceanside, CA: Second Renaissance Books, 1991.)

The Ayn Rand Lexicon: Objectivism from A to Z. Edited by Harry Binswanger. New York: Meridian, 1988. (Hardcover: New York: NAL Books, 1986.)

Capitalism: The Unknown Ideal. New York: Signet, 1967. (Hardcover: New York: New American Library, 1966.)

For the New Intellectual. New York: Signet, 1963. (Hardcover: New York: Random House, 1961.)

Introduction to Objectivist Epistemology, Expanded Second Edition. Edited by Harry Binswanger and Leonard Peikoff. New York: Meridian, 1990. (First Edition: New York: The Objectivist, Inc., 1967.)

Philosophy: Who Needs It. New York: Signet, 1984. (Hardcover: New York: Bobbs-Merrill, 1982.)

Return of the Primitive: The Anti-Industrial Revolution, New Expanded Edition of *The New Left: The Anti-Industrial Revolution*. Edited by Peter Schwartz. New York: Meridian, 1999. (First Edition: New York: Signet, 1971.)

The Romantic Manifesto, Second Revised Edition. New York: Signet, 1975. (First Edition, Hardcover: Cleveland: World Publishing, 1969.)

The Virtue of Selfishness. New York: Signet, 1964. Please note: although technically the same edition, this book was re-typeset in 1994. Page numbers refer to printings 32 and later. (Hardcover: New York: NAL, 1964.)

The Voice of Reason: Essays in Objectivist Thought. Edited by Leonard Peikoff. New York: Meridian, 1990. (Hardcover: New York: NAL Books, 1989.)

Why Businessmen Need Philosophy. Edited by Richard E. Ralston. Los Angeles, CA: The Ayn Rand Institute Press, 1999.

"*Playboy*'s Interview with Ayn Rand" pamphlet. Gaylordsville, CT: Second Renaissance Books. (*Playboy*, Mar. 1964.)

By Leonard Peikoff

Objectivism: The Philosophy of Ayn Rand. New York: Meridian, 1993. (Hardcover: New York: Dutton, 1991.)

The Ominous Parallels. New York: Meridian, 1993. (Hardcover: New York: Stein and Day, 1982.)

"Founders of Western Philosophy: Thales to Hume" taped lecture series (1972). Sold as "The History of Philosophy, Volume I." Gaylordsville, CT: Second Renaissance Books, 1994.

"Introduction to Logic" taped lecture series (1974). Gaylordsville, CT: Second Renaissance Books, 1993.

"Philosophy of Education" taped lecture series (1985). Gaylordsville, CT: Second Renaissance Books, 1985.

"Poems I Like—and Why" taped lecture series (1999). Gaylordsville, CT: Second Renaissance Books, 2000.

"Understanding Objectivism" taped lecture series (1984). Gaylordsville, CT: Second Renaissance Books, 1993.

By Harry Binswanger

The Biological Basis of Teleological Concepts. Irvine, California: The
Ayn Rand Institute Press, 1990.

"Volition as Cognitive Self-Regulation" booklet. Irvine, California:
The Ayn Rand Bookstore, 2008. (*Organizational Behavior and
Human Decision Processes,* Vol. 50, 154–178, 1991.)

"How to Study Ayn Rand's Writings" taped lecture (1994). Irvine,
California: The Ayn Rand Bookstore, 2008.

Periodicals:

The Ayn Rand Letter (1971–1976).* Santa Ana, California:
The Ayn Rand Institute eStore, 2021. **estore.aynrand.org**

The Intellectual Activist (1979–1991), Lincroft, NJ: *TIA* Publications, Inc.
Available at **https://estore.aynrand.org/search?q=The+
Intellectual+Activist**

The Intellectual Activist (1992–1997)

The Objectivist Forum (1980–1987).* New York: TOF Publications, 1993.
Available at **tofpublications.com/tof/**

The Objectivist Newsletter (1962–1965).* Santa Ana, California:
The Ayn Rand Institute eStore, 2021. **estore.aynrand.org**

*Bound volume

ABBREVIATIONS

The following abbreviations are used throughout the glossary:

AR   Ayn Rand
ARC   *The Ayn Rand Column*
ARL   *The Ayn Rand Letter*
BBTC   *The Biological Basis of Teleological Concepts*
CUI   *Capitalism: The Unknown Ideal*
FNI   *For the New Intellectual*
GS   "This Is John Galt Speaking" (Galt's Speech) from *Atlas Shrugged* (1957), reprinted in *FNI*
HB   Harry Binswanger
ITOE   *Introduction to Objectivist Epistemology*
LEX   *The Ayn Rand Lexicon: Objectivism from A to Z*
LP   Leonard Peikoff
OED   *Oxford English Dictionary*
OP   *The Ominous Parallels*
OPAR   *Objectivism: The Philosophy of Ayn Rand*
PLB   "*Playboy*'s Interview with Ayn Rand" pamphlet
PWNI   *Philosophy: Who Needs It*
Q&A   Question & Answer period from the lecture
RM   *The Romantic Manifesto*
ROP   *Return of the Primitive: The Anti-Industrial Revolution*
TIA   *The Intellectual Activist*
TOF   *The Objectivist Forum*
TON   *The Objectivist Newsletter*
VOR   *The Voice of Reason: Essays in Objectivist Thought*
VOS   *The Virtue of Selfishness*
WBNP   *Why Businessmen Need Philosophy*

GLOSSARY

Absolute

"**Absolute**" in this context means necessitated by the nature of existence and, therefore, unchangeable by human (or any other) agency.

LP, "The Metaphysically Given as Absolute," *OPAR*, 24.

Abstraction

"**Abstraction**" is . . . the power to separate mentally and make cognitive use of an aspect of reality that cannot exist separately.

LP, "Differentiation and Integration as the Means to a Unit-Perspective," *OPAR*, 78.

Altruism

The basic principle of **altruism** is that man has no right to exist for his own sake, that service to others is the only justification of his existence, and that self-sacrifice is his highest moral duty, virtue and value . . . which means: the *self* as a standard of evil, the *selfless* as a standard of the good.

AR, "Faith and Force: The Destroyers of the Modern World," *PWNI*, 61.

Ambition

"**Ambition**" means the systematic pursuit of achievement and of constant improvement in respect to one's goal.

AR, "Tax-Credits for Education," *ARL*, Mar. 13, 1972, 51.

Anarchism

Anarchism is the idea that there should be no government.

LP, "Statism as the Politics of Unreason," *OPAR*, 371.

"Anti-Concept" | An **anti-concept** is an unnecessary and rationally unusable term designed to replace and obliterate some legitimate concept.

AR, "Credibility and Polarization," *ARL*, Oct. 11, 1971, 1.

Appeasement | **Appeasement** is not consideration for the feelings of others, it is *consideration for and compliance with the unjust, irrational and evil feelings of others.*

AR, "The Age of Envy," *ROP*, 136.

Arbitrary | An **arbitrary** claim is one for which there is no evidence, either perceptual or conceptual.

LP, "The Arbitrary as Neither True Nor False," *OPAR*, 164.

Argument from Intimidation | The psychological pressure method consists of threatening to impeach an opponent's character by means of his argument, thus impeaching the argument without debate . . . and may be designated as "**the argument from intimidation**."

AR, "The Argument from Intimidation," *VOS*, 162.

Art | **Art** is a selective re-creation of reality according to an artist's metaphysical value-judgments.

AR, "The Psycho-Epistemology of Art," *RM*, 19. LP discusses in "Art as a Concretization of Metaphysics," *OPAR*, 417.

Axiom | An **axiom** is a statement that identifies the base of knowledge and of any further statement pertaining to that knowledge, a statement necessarily contained in all others.

AR, GS, *FNI*, 155. LP discusses in "Existence, Consciousness, and Identity as the Basic Axioms," *OPAR*, 11.

Axiomatic Concept	An **axiomatic concept** is the identification of a primary fact of reality, which cannot be analyzed, i.e., reduced to other facts or broken into component parts. It is implicit in all facts and in all knowledge. AR, "Axiomatic Concepts," *ITOE*, 55. LP discusses in "Existence, Consciousness, and Identity as the Basic Axioms," *OPAR*, 7.
Benevolent Universe Premise	The "**benevolent universe**" **premise** [means] . . . reality is "benevolent" in the sense that if you *do* adapt to it—i.e., if you do think, value, and act rationally—then you can (and barring accidents you will) achieve your values. . . . Success and happiness are the metaphysically to-be-expected. LP, "The Philosophy of Objectivism" lecture series (1976), Lecture 8, quoted in "Benevolent Universe Premise," *LEX*, 51. Last sentence is taken from earlier in the passage. [*See* **Malevolent Universe Premise**.]
"Borderline-Case"	The "**borderline-case**" **problem** [is the question:] where . . . does one draw the line in grouping concretes that are neither essentially the same . . . nor essentially different? LP, "Concepts as Objective," *OPAR*, 115.
Capitalism	**Capitalism** is a social system based on the recognition of individual rights, including property rights, in which all property is privately owned. AR, "What Is Capitalism?" *CUI*, 19. LP discusses in "Capitalism as the Only Moral Social System," *OPAR*, 380.

Causality, Law of	The **law of causality** is . . . [that] the nature of an action is caused and determined by the nature of the entities that act; a thing cannot act in contradiction to its nature. AR, GS, *FNI*, 151. LP discusses in "Causality as a Corollary of Identity," *OPAR*, 15.
Causation, Final	[*See* **Final Causation**.]
Censorship	**Censorship** . . . is a government edict that forbids the discussion of some specific subjects or ideas . . . an edict enforced by the government's scrutiny of all forms of communication prior to their public release. AR, "Have Gun, Will Nudge," *TON*, Mar. 1962, 9.
Central Purpose	A **central purpose** is the long-range goal that constitutes the primary claimant on a man's time, energy, and resources. LP, "Productiveness as the Adjustment of Nature to Man," *OPAR*, 299. [*See also* **Purpose**.]
Certain	A conclusion is "**certain**" when the evidence in its favor is conclusive; i.e., when it has been logically validated. LP, "Certainty as Contextual," *OPAR*, 179. [*See* **Possible**, **Probable**.]
Character	"**Character**" means a man's nature or identity insofar as this is shaped by the moral values he accepts and automatizes. LP, "The Philosophy of Objectivism" lecture series (1976), Q&A Lecture 2, quoted in "Character," *LEX*, 68.

Characterization	**Characterization** [in literature] is the portrayal of those essential traits which form the unique, distinctive personality of an individual human being. AR, "Basic Principles of Literature," *RM*, 87.
Coercion	[*See* **Physical Force.**]
Collectivism	**Collectivism** is the theory that . . . the collective—society, the community, the nation, the proletariat, the race, etc.—is *the unit of reality and the standard of value.* LP, "The Cause of Nazism," *OP*, 17. [*See* **Individualism.**]
Common Sense	**Common sense** is a simple and non-self-conscious use of logic. [Extemporaneous, unedited formulation.] AR, answering question during LP, "The Philosophy of Objectivism" lecture series (1976), Q&A Lecture 11, quoted in "Common Sense," *LEX*, 77.
Communism	"**Communism** [is] a theory or system of social organization based on the holding of all property in common, actual ownership being ascribed to the community as a whole or to the state." *The American College Dictionary*, quoted in AR, "The Dying Victim of Berlin," *ARC*, 38.
Competition, Economic	**Economic competition** is a rivalry in producing and offering values. HB, "'Buy American' Is Un-American," *WBNP*, 147.

Complex	The "**complex**" is that which involves *many* elements or units, all tied together or interrelated. LP, "Why Should One Act on Principle?" *TIA*, Feb. 27, 1989, 3. [*See* **Simple**.]
Compromise	A **compromise** is an adjustment of conflicting claims by mutual concessions. . . . It is only in regard to concretes or particulars, implementing a mutually accepted basic principle, that one may compromise. AR, "Doesn't Life Require Compromise?" *VOS*, 79. LP discusses in "Integrity as Loyalty to Rational Principles," *OPAR*, 262.
Concept	A **concept** is a mental integration of two or more units possessing the same distinguishing characteristic(s), with their particular measurements omitted. AR, "Concept-Formation," *ITOE*, 13. LP discusses in "Concept-Formation as a Mathematical Process," *OPAR*, 88. [*See also* **First-Level Concept, Invalid Concept**.]
Conceptual Common Denominator	The "**Conceptual Common Denominator**" [is] . . . "the characteristic(s) reducible to a unit of measurement, by means of which man differentiates two or more existents from other existents possessing it." AR, "Concept-Formation," *ITOE*, 15. LP discusses in "Concept-Formation as a Mathematical Process," *OPAR*, 87.

Concretization	**Concretization** is an epistemological process, in which, to clarify some theory, you provide a concrete example. [Extemporaneous, unedited formulation.] LP, "Founders of Western Philosophy: Thales to Hume" lecture series (1972), Q&A Lecture 11.
Conjunctions	**Conjunctions** . . . are concepts denoting relation-ships among thoughts ("and," "but," "or," etc.). AR, "Concepts of Consciousness," *ITOE*, 37.
Consciousness	**Consciousness** [is] the faculty of perceiving that which exists. [Axiomatic concept: not a definition.] AR, GS, *FNI*, 124. LP discusses in "Existence, Consciousness, and Identity as the Basic Axioms," *OPAR*, 6.
Context	[1] The **context** is the entire field of a mind's awareness or knowledge at any level of its cognitive development. AR, "Definitions," *ITOE*, 43. LP discusses in "Definition as the Final Step in Concept-Formation," *OPAR*, 97. [2] "**Context**" means "the sum of cognitive elements conditioning an item of knowledge." LP, "Knowledge as Contextual," *OPAR*, 123.
Contradiction, Law of	[*See* **Non-Contradiction, Law of.**]
Corollary	A "**corollary**" is a self-evident implication of already established knowledge. LP, "Causality as a Corollary of Identity," *OPAR*, 15.

Cowardice, Moral   **Moral cowardice** is fear of upholding the good *because* it is good, and fear of opposing the evil *because* it is evil.

AR, "Altruism as Appeasement," *VOR*, 37.

Creation   "**Creation**" means the power to bring into existence an arrangement (or combination or integration) of natural elements that had not existed before.

AR, "The Metaphysical Versus the Man-Made," *PWNI*, 25.
LP discusses in "The Metaphysically Given as Absolute," *OPAR*, 25.

Crime   A **crime** is a violation of the right(s) of other men by force (or fraud).

AR, "'Political' Crimes," *ROP*, 176.

"Crow Epistemology"   The "**crow epistemology**" [refers to] the fact that any consciousness—animal or human—can deal mentally with only so many units [in one frame of awareness].

[Extemporaneous, unedited formulation. The fact was discovered first in an experiment with crows.]

AR, "The Role of Words," *ITOE*, 172. The bracketed text "in one frame of awareness" is in the published version.

[*See* **Unit-Economy**.]

Culture   A nation's **culture** is the sum of the intellectual achievements of individual men, which their fellow-citizens have accepted in whole or in part, and which have influenced the nation's way of life.

AR, "Don't Let It Go," *PWNI*, 205–206.

Deduction	**Deduction** is . . . the process of applying a universal or general proposition to a particular case. . . . [It] is the process of reasoning from a universal premise to a conclusion which is no wider in extent . . . than the premises. [Extemporaneous, unedited formulation.] LP, "Introduction to Logic" lecture series (1974), Lecture 4. [*See* **Induction**.]
Definition	A **definition** is a statement that identifies the nature of the units subsumed under a concept. AR, "Definitions," *ITOE*, 40.
Democracy	"**Democracy**" means a [political] system of unlimited majority rule. LP, "Government as an Agency to Protect Rights," *OPAR*, 368.
Deserve	To "**deserve**" . . . is to "become worthy of recompense (i.e., reward or punishment), according to the good or ill of character or conduct." *OED*, quoted in LP, "Justice as Rationality in the Evaluation of Men," *OPAR*, 282–283.
Determinism	**Determinism** is the theory that everything that happens in the universe—including every thought, feeling, and action of man—is necessitated by previous factors, so that nothing could ever have happened differently from the way it did, and everything in the future is already pre-set and inevitable. LP, "The Philosophy of Objectivism" lecture series (1976), Lecture 1, quoted in "Determinism," *LEX*, 122. [*See also* **Indeterminism**.]

Dictatorship   A **dictatorship** is a country that does not recognize individual rights, whose government holds total, unlimited power over men. . . . [It] has four characteristics: one-party rule, executions without trial for political offenses, expropriation or nationalization of private property, and censorship.

AR, PLB, 15.

Differentiation   "**Differentiation**" is the process of grasping differences, i.e., of distinguishing one or more objects of awareness from the others.

LP, "Differentiation and Integration as the Means to a Unit-Perspective," OPAR, 77.

[See **Integration**.]

Dogma   A **dogma** is a set of beliefs accepted on faith: that is, without rational justification or against rational evidence.

AR, PLB, 9.

"Duty"   "**Duty**" [means] the moral necessity to perform certain actions for no reason other than obedience to some higher authority, without regard to any personal goal, motive, desire or interest.

[Invalid concept.]

AR, "Causality Versus Duty," PWNI, 96. LP discusses in "Values as Objective," OPAR, 245.

Economic Growth	**"Economic growth"** means the rise of an economy's productivity, due to the discovery of new knowledge, new products, new techniques, which means: due to the achievements of men's productive ability. AR, "Progress or Sacrifice," *ARC*, 9.
Economic Power	**Economic power** [as opposed to political power] . . . is the power to produce and to trade what one has produced. . . . [It] is exercised by means of a *positive*, by offering men a reward, an incentive, a payment, a value. AR, "America's Persecuted Minority: Big Business," *CUI*, 47–48. There is a significant deletion in the excerpt. For a similar treatment, see LP, "Capitalism as the System of Objectivity," *OPAR*, 402. [*See* **Political Power.**]
Education	**Education** [is] the systematic training of the conceptual faculty of the young by means of supplying in essentials both its content and method. [Extemporaneous, unedited formulation.] LP, "Philosophy of Education" lecture series (1985), Lecture 1.
Effort	**"Effort"** means the expenditure of energy to achieve a purpose. LP, "The Primary Choice as the Choice to Focus or Not," *OPAR*, 59.
Ego	[*See* **Self.**]

Egoism	**Egoism** states that each man's primary moral obligation is to achieve his own welfare, well-being, or self-interest. . . . He should be "selfish" in the sense of being the beneficiary of his own moral actions. LP, "The Individual as the Proper Beneficiary of His Own Moral Action," *OPAR*, 230.
Egoistic	"**Egoistic**" . . . means self-sustaining by an act of choice and as a matter of principle. LP, "The Individual as the Proper Beneficiary of His Own Moral Action," *OPAR*, 231.
Emergency	An **emergency** is an unchosen, unexpected event, limited in time, that creates conditions under which human survival is impossible—such as a flood, an earthquake, a fire, a shipwreck. AR, "The Ethics of Emergencies," *VOS*, 54.
Emotions	**Emotions** are the automatic results of man's value judgments integrated by his subconscious; emotions are estimates of that which furthers man's values or threatens them, that which is *for* him or *against* him. AR, "The Objectivist Ethics," *VOS*, 30.
Entity	Since it is axiomatic, the referents of [**entity**] can be specified only ostensively, by pointing to the things given to men in sense perception . . . solid things with a perceivable shape, such as a rock, a person, or a table. [Axiomatic concept: not a definition.] LP, "Causality as a Corollary of Identity," *OPAR*, 13.

Epistemology	**Epistemology** is a science devoted to the discovery of the proper methods of acquiring and validating knowledge. AR, "Concepts of Consciousness," *ITOE*, 36.
Essential Characteristic	The "**essential**" **characteristic(s)** is the fundamental characteristic(s) which makes the units the kind of existents they are and differentiates them from all other known existents. LP, "Definition as the Final Step in Concept-Formation," *OPAR*, 97.
Esthetics	**Esthetics** [is the branch of philosophy that] studies the nature of art and defines the standards by which an art work should be judged. LP, Introduction to "Reality," *OPAR*, 3.
Ethics	**Ethics** is the branch of philosophy that . . . provides "a code of values to guide man's choice and actions—the choices and actions that determine the purpose and the course of his life." LP, Introduction to "The Good," *OPAR*, 206, quoting AR, "The Objectivist Ethics," *VOS*, 13. [*See* **Morality**.]
Evaluation	An **evaluation** is an identification of the beneficial or harmful relationship of something to a value. HB, Seminar on *OPAR*, Objectivist Graduate Center, Fall 1994.

Evasion	**Evasion** . . . is "the act of blanking out, the willful suspension of one's consciousness, the refusal to think—not blindness, but the refusal to see; not ignorance, but the refusal to know."
	LP, "The Primary Choice as the Choice to Focus or Not," *OPAR*, 61, quoting AR, GS, *FNI*, 127.
Evidence	"**Evidence**" . . . is "testimony or facts tending to prove or disprove any conclusion."
	OED, quoted in LP, "Certainty as Contextual," *OPAR*, 176.
Evil	[*See* **Standard of Value**.]
Excluded Middle, Law of	Formulated and named by Aristotle, the **Law of Excluded Middle** states: everything is either A or non-A at a given time and in a given respect.
	[Extemporaneous, unedited formulation.]
	Aristotle, formulated in LP, "Introduction to Logic" lecture series (1974), Lecture 1.
Existence	"**Existence**" here is a collective noun, denoting the sum of existents.
	[Axiomatic concept: not a definition.]
	LP, "Existence, Consciousness, and Identity as the Basic Axioms," *OPAR*, 4.
Existent	An "**existent**" [is] something that exists, be it a thing, an attribute or an action.
	[Axiomatic concept: not a definition.]
	AR, "Cognition and Measurement," *ITOE*, 5.

Extortion	**Extortion** . . . consists of obtaining material values, not in exchange for values, but by the threat of force, violence or injury. AR, "The Nature of Government," *VOS*, 130; *CUI*, 333.
Extrospection	**Extrospection** is a process of cognition directed outward—a process of apprehending some existent(s) of the external world. AR, "Concepts of Consciousness," *ITOE*, 29. [*See* **Introspection**.]
Faith	"**Faith**" means acceptance on the basis of feeling rather than of evidence. LP, "Mysticism and Skepticism as Denials of Reason," *OPAR*, 183.
Fallacy of "Package-Dealing"	"**Package-Dealing**" is the **fallacy** of failing to discriminate crucial differences. It consists of treating together, as parts of a single conceptual whole or "package," elements which differ essentially in nature, truth-status, importance or value. LP footnote in AR, "The Metaphysical Versus the Man-Made," *PWNI*, 24.
Fallacy of Reification of the Zero	A **fallacy** I call the **reification of the zero** . . . consists of regarding "nothing" as a *thing*, as a special, different kind of *existent*. AR, "Axiomatic Concepts," *ITOE*, 60.

Fallacy of "Rewriting Reality"	The attempt to alter the metaphysically given is . . . the **fallacy of "rewriting reality."** Those who commit it regard metaphysically given facts as nonabsolute and, therefore, feel free to imagine an alternative to them. In effect, they regard the universe as being merely a first draft of reality, which anyone may decide at will to rewrite. LP, "The Metaphysically Given as Absolute," *OPAR*, 26–27.
Fallacy of Self-Exclusion	The **fallacy of self-exclusion** is a form of self-refutation in which what a statement asserts is contradicted by the very act of asserting the statement, e.g., "There is no truth." HB, Seminar on Logic, Objectivist Graduate Center, Spring 1995.
Fallacy of the "Frozen Abstraction"	"The **fallacy of the frozen abstraction**" . . . consists of substituting some one particular concrete for the wider abstract class to which it belongs . . . [e.g.,] substituting a specific ethics (altruism) for the wider abstraction of "ethics." AR, "Collectivized Ethics," *VOS*, 94.
Fallacy of the "Stolen Concept"	The **fallacy of the "stolen concept"** . . . consists in using a higher-level concept while denying or ignoring its hierarchical roots, i.e., one or more of the earlier concepts on which it logically depends. LP, "Knowledge as Hierarchical," *OPAR*, 136.

False, the   "True" and "false" are assessments within the field
                        of human cognition: they designate a relationship
                        [of] correspondence or contradiction between an
                        idea and reality. . . . **The false** is established as
                        false by reference to a body of evidence and within
                        a context, and is pronounced false because it
                        contradicts the evidence.

                        LP, "The Philosophy of Objectivism" lecture series (1976),
                        Lecture 6, quoted in "Falsehood," *LEX*, 158. Brackets and
                        ellipses appear in the published version.

Fascism   **Fascism** is: "a governmental system with strong
                        centralized power, permitting no opposition or
                        criticism, controlling all affairs of the nation
                        (industrial, commercial, etc.), emphasizing an
                        aggressive nationalism."

                        The American College Dictionary, quoted in AR, "The Fascist New
                        Frontier," *ARC*, 98.

Femininity   For a woman *qua* woman, the essence of **femininity**
                        is hero worship—the desire to look up to man.

                        AR, "About a Woman President," *VOR*, 268.

Final Causation   Aristotelian **final causation** (which, in fact, applies
                        only to a conscious being) [is] the process by which
                        an end determines the means, i.e., the process of
                        choosing a goal and taking the actions necessary to
                        achieve it.

                        AR, "Causality Versus Duty," *PWNI*, 99.

First-Level Concept	A **"first-level" concept**, such as "table" or "man," is one formed directly from perceptual data. LP, "Concepts of Consciousness as Involving Measurement-Omission," *OPAR*, 91.
"Floating Abstractions"	**"Floating abstractions"** [are] . . . concepts detached from existents, concepts that a person takes over from other men without knowing what specific units the concepts denote. LP, "Definition as the Final Step in Concept-Formation," *OPAR*, 96.
Focus	**"Focus"** is the state of a goal-directed mind committed to attaining full awareness of reality. LP, "The Primary Choice as the Choice to Focus or Not," *OPAR*, 56.
Force	[*See* **Physical Force.**]
Fraud	**Fraud** . . . consists of obtaining material values without their owner's consent, under false pretenses or false promises. AR, "The Nature of Government," *VOS*, 130; *CUI*, 333.
Free	A course of thought or action is **"free,"** if it is selected from two or more courses possible under the circumstances. LP, "The Primary Choice as the Choice to Focus or Not," *OPAR*, 55.
Free Speech	[*See* **Right of Free Speech.**]

Free Will	"**Free will**" is your mind's freedom to think or not, the only will you have, your only freedom, the choice that controls all the choices you make and determines your life and your character. [Axiomatic concept: not a definition.] AR, GS, *FNI*, 127. [Same as "volition." *See* **Volition**.]
Freedom	**Freedom**, in a political context, has only one meaning: *the absence of physical coercion*. AR, "America's Persecuted Minority: Big Business," *CUI*, 46.
"Frozen Abstraction"	[*See* **Fallacy of the "Frozen Abstraction."**]
Fundamental	"**Fundamental**" means that upon which everything in a given context depends. LP, "'Life' as the Essential Root of 'Value,'" *OPAR*, 209.
Fundamentality, Rule of	The **rule of fundamentality** [states that] when a given group of existents has more than one characteristic distinguishing it from other existents, man must observe the relationships among these various characteristics and discover the one on which all the others (or the greatest number of others) depend, i.e., the fundamental characteristic without which the others would not be possible. This fundamental characteristic is the *essential* distinguishing characteristic of the existents involved, and the proper *defining* characteristic of the concept. AR, "Definitions," *ITOE*, 45.

Goal-Directed	**"Goal-directed**," in this context, [designates] the fact that the automatic functions of living organisms are actions whose nature is such that they *result* in the preservation of an organism's life. AR, footnote in "The Objectivist Ethics," *VOS*, 17. LP discusses in "Living Organisms as Goal-Directed and Conditional," *OPAR*, 190.
Good	[*See* **Standard of Value.**] [*See also* **Objective Theory of the Good.**]
Government	A **government** is an institution that holds the exclusive power to *enforce* certain rules of social conduct in a given geographical area. AR, "The Nature of Government," *VOS*, 125; *CUI*, 329. LP discusses in "Government as an Agency to Protect Rights," *OPAR*, 363.
Grammar	**Grammar** is a science dealing with the formulation of the proper methods of verbal expression and communication, i.e., the methods of organizing words (concepts) into sentences. AR, "Concepts of Consciousness," *ITOE*, 37.
Happiness	**Happiness** is that state of consciousness which proceeds from the achievement of one's values. AR, GS, *FNI*, 123. LP discusses in "Happiness as the Normal Condition of Man," *OPAR*, 336.
Happiness, Right to the Pursuit of	[*See* **Right to the Pursuit of Happiness.**]

Hatred of the Good for Being the Good	**Hatred of the good for being the good** means hatred of that which one regards as good by one's own (conscious or subconscious) judgment. It means hatred of a person for possessing a value or virtue one regards as desirable. AR, "The Age of Envy," *ROP*, 131.
Hedonism	**Hedonism** is the doctrine which holds that the good is whatever gives you pleasure and, therefore, pleasure is the standard of morality. AR, PLB, 8.
Hierarchy of Knowledge	A **hierarchy of knowledge** means a body of concepts and conclusions ranked in order of logical dependence, one upon another, according to each item's distance from the base of the structure. The base is the perceptual data with which cognition begins. LP, "Knowledge as Hierarchical," *OPAR*, 131.
Honesty	"**Honesty**" is the refusal to fake reality, i.e., to pretend that facts are other than they are. LP, "Honesty as the Rejection of Unreality," *OPAR*, 267.
Hostility	Caused by a profound self-doubt, self-condemnation, and fear, **hostility** is a type of projection that directs toward other people the hatred which the hostile person feels toward himself. AR, "The Psychology of Psychologizing," *VOR*, 25.

Humor	**Humor** is the denial of metaphysical importance to that which you laugh at. AR, answering question during LP, "The Philosophy of Objectivism" lecture series (1976), Q&A Lecture 11, quoted in "Humor," *LEX*, 207.
Idealism	**Idealism** [as a technical term in philosophy] . . . is the view . . . from metaphysics, that reality is basically non-material; that the material world is not an irreducible primary, but actually simply a by-product or expression of something more fundamental, something which is non-material in character. [Extemporaneous, unedited formulation.] LP, "Founders of Western Philosophy: Thales to Hume" lecture series (1972), Lecture 2. [*See* **Materialism**.]
Identity	The "**identity**" of an existent means that which it is, the sum of its attributes or characteristics. [Axiomatic concept: not a definition.] LP, "Existence, Consciousness, and Identity as the Basic Axioms," *OPAR*, 6.
Identity, Law of	The **Law of Identity** [states]: to be is to be something, to have a nature, to possess *identity*. A thing is itself; or, in the traditional formula, A is A. LP, "Existence, Consciousness, and Identity as the Basic Axioms," *OPAR*, 6.

Ideology, Political	A **political ideology** is a set of principles aimed at establishing or maintaining a certain social system. AR, "The Wreckage of the Consensus," *CUI*, 222.
Imagination	Man's **imagination** is nothing more than the ability to rearrange the things he has observed in reality. AR, "The Metaphysical Versus the Man-Made," *PWNI*, 25.
Implicit Knowledge	**Implicit knowledge** is passively held material which, to be grasped, requires a special focus and process of consciousness. AR, "Axiomatic Concepts," *ITOE*, 57.
Important	"**Important**" . . . means "a quality, character or standing such as to entitle to attention or consideration." *The American College Dictionary*, quoted in AR, "Philosophy and Sense of Life," *RM*, 28. LP discusses in "Art as a Concretization of Metaphysics," *OPAR*, 424.
Inalienable	**Inalienable** means that which we may not take away, suspend, infringe, restrict or violate—not ever, not at any time, not for any purpose whatsoever. AR, "Textbook of Americanism," *ARC*, 92.
Independence	One's acceptance of the responsibility of forming one's own judgments and of living by the work of one's own mind . . . is the virtue of **independence**. AR, "The Objectivist Ethics," *VOS*, 28. LP discusses in "Independence as a Primary Orientation to Reality, Not to Other Men," *OPAR*, 251.

Indeterminism   **Indeterminism** . . . holds that not all human action is necessitated, because some actions allegedly have no causes at all. . . . In certain cases it is just a sheer, causeless accident which of two actions a man performs.

HB, "Volition as Cognitive Self-Regulation" booklet, 5.

Individual Rights   [*See* **Right**.]

Individualism   "**Individualism**" is the view that, in social issues, the individual is the unit of value; this is a moral corollary of the principle that each man is an end in himself.

LP, "Individual Rights as Absolutes," *OPAR*, 361.

[*See* **Collectivism**.]

Induction   An Aristotelian definition of **induction** [is] the process of reasoning from the observation of concretes or individuals to a general or universal conclusion.

[Extemporaneous, unedited formulation.]

LP, "Introduction to Logic" lecture series (1974), Lecture 9.

[*See* **Deduction**.]

Infinity   "**Infinity**" denotes merely a potentiality of indefinite addition or subdivision.

LP, "Idealism and Materialism as the Rejection of Basic Axioms," *OPAR*, 31.

Inflation	"**Inflation**" is defined in the dictionary as "undue expansion or increase of the currency of a country, esp. by the issuing of paper money not redeemable in specie."
	Random House Dictionary, quoted in AR, "Moral Inflation," *ARL*, Mar. 11, 1974, 301.
Initiation of Physical Force	"**Initiation**" [**of physical force**] means *starting* the use of force against an innocent individual(s), one who has not himself started its use against others.
	LP, "The Initiation of Physical Force as Evil," *OPAR*, 310.
"Instinct"	An "**instinct**" is an unerring and automatic form of knowledge.
	[Invalid concept.]
	AR, GS, *FNI*, 121–122.
Integration	"**Integration**" is the process of uniting elements into an inseparable whole.
	LP, "Differentiation and Integration as the Means to a Unit-Perspective," *OPAR*, 77.
	[*See* **Differentiation**.]
Integrity	"**Integrity**" is loyalty in action to one's convictions and values.
	LP, "Integrity as Loyalty to Rational Principles," *OPAR*, 259.
Intellectuals	**Intellectuals** [are] those who disseminate ideas and whose professional work lies in the field of the humanities.
	AR, "The Age of Envy," *ROP*, 150.

Intelligence	**Intelligence** is the ability to deal with a broad range of abstractions. AR, "The Comprachicos," *ROP*, 58.
Intrinsic Theory of Concepts	[Certain] schools of thought regard the referents of **concepts** as **intrinsic**, i.e., as "universals" inherent in things . . . as special existents unrelated to man's consciousness—to be perceived by man directly, like any other kind of concrete existents, but perceived by some non-sensory or extra-sensory means. AR, "Definitions," *ITOE*, 53. [*See* **Subjective Theory of Concepts**.] [*See also* **Objective**.]
Intrinsic Theory of the Good	The **intrinsic theory** holds that the **good** is inherent in certain things or actions as such, regardless of their context and consequences, regardless of any benefit or injury they may cause to the actors and subjects involved. AR, "What Is Capitalism?" *CUI*, 21. [*See* **Objective Theory of the Good, Subjectivist Theory of the Good**.]
Introspection	**Introspection** is a process of cognition directed inward—a process of apprehending one's own psychological actions in regard to some existent(s) of the external world, such actions as thinking, feeling, reminiscing, etc. AR, "Concepts of Consciousness," *ITOE*, 29. [*See* **Extrospection**.]

Invalid Concept	**Invalid concepts** [are] words that represent attempts to integrate errors, contradictions or false propositions, such as concepts originating in mysticism—or words without specific definitions, without referents, which can mean anything to anyone, such as modern "anti-concepts." AR, "Definitions," *ITOE*, 49. LP discusses in "Knowledge as Hierarchical," *OPAR*, 137.
Irrationalism	"**Irrationalism**" is the doctrine that reason is not a valid means of knowledge or a proper guide to action. LP, "Hitler's War Against Reason," *OP*, 47.
Irreducible Primary	An **irreducible primary** is a fact which cannot be analyzed (i.e., broken into components) or derived from antecedent facts. AR, "Philosophical Detection," *PWNI*, 13.
Judge	To **judge** means: to evaluate a given concrete by reference to an abstract principle or standard. AR, "How Does One Lead a Rational Life in an Irrational Society?" *VOS*, 84.
Justice	"**Justice**" is the virtue of judging men's character and conduct objectively and of acting accordingly, granting to each man that which he deserves. LP, "Justice as Rationality in the Evaluation of Men," *OPAR*, 276.

Knowledge	"**Knowledge**" is . . . a mental grasp of a fact(s) of reality, reached either by perceptual observation or by a process of reason based on perceptual observation.
	AR, "Concepts of Consciousness," *ITOE*, 35. LP discusses in "Mysticism and Skepticism as Denials of Reason," *OPAR*, 182.
	[*See also* **Implicit Knowledge**.]
Language	**Language** is a code of visual-auditory symbols that serves the psycho-epistemological function of converting concepts into the mental equivalent of concretes.
	AR, "Concept-Formation," *ITOE*, 10. LP discusses in "Differentiation and Integration as the Means to a Unit-Perspective," *OPAR*, 79.
Law	A "**law**" is a rule of social conduct enforced by the government.
	HB, "What Is Objective Law?" *TIA*, Jan. 1992, 8.
Law of Causality	[*See* **Causality, Law of**.]
Law of Excluded Middle	[*See* **Excluded Middle, Law of**.]
Law of Identity	[*See* **Identity, Law of**.]
Law of Non-Contradiction	[*See* **Non-Contradiction, Law of**.]
Liberty, Right to	[*See* **Right to Liberty**.]

Life	**Life** is a process of self-sustaining and self-generated action.
	AR, GS, *FNI*, 121. LP discusses in "Living Organisms as Goal-Directed and Conditional," *OPAR*, 191.
Life, Right to	[*See* **Right to Life.**]
Literature	**Literature** [is the branch of art which] re-creates reality by means of language.
	AR, "Art and Cognition," *RM*, 46.
Lobbying	"**Lobbying**" is the activity of attempting to influence legislation by privately influencing the legislators.
	AR, "The Pull Peddlers," *CUI*, 168; *VOR*, 262.
Logic	**Logic** is the art of *non-contradictory identification*.
	AR, GS, *FNI*, 126. LP discusses in "Objectivity as Volitional Adherence to Reality by the Method of Logic," *OPAR*, 118. See elaboration in LP, "Knowledge as Hierarchical," *OPAR*, 138.
Long-Range	"**Long-range**" means "allowing for or extending into the more distant future."
	The Random House Dictionary of the English Language, quoted in LP, "Man's Life as the Standard of Moral Value," *OPAR*, 214.
Love	"**Love**" is . . . an emotion proceeding from the evaluation of an existent as a positive value and as a source of pleasure.
	AR, "Concepts of Consciousness," *ITOE*, 34.

Malevolent Universe Premise	A "**malevolent universe**" metaphysics [is] the theory that man, by his very nature, is helpless and doomed—that success, happiness, achievement are impossible to him. AR, "The Ethics of Emergencies," *VOS*, 56. [*See* **Benevolent Universe Premise**.]
Man	**Man** is the rational animal. Aristotle. AR discusses in "Definitions," *ITOE*, 44.
Man-Made	"**Man-made** facts" [are] objects, institutions, practices, or rules of conduct that are of human origin. LP, "The Metaphysically Given as Absolute," *OPAR*, 24. [*See* **Metaphysically Given**.]
Man's Survival qua Man	"**Man's survival qua man**" means the terms, methods, conditions and goals required for the survival of a rational being through the whole of his lifespan—in all those aspects of existence which are open to his choice. AR, "The Objectivist Ethics," *VOS*, 26. LP discusses in "Man's Life as the Standard of Moral Value," *OPAR*, 219. [*See* **Standard of Value**.]
Market Value	[*See* **Socially Objective Value**.]

Materialism	**Materialism** [as a technical term in philosophy] . . . is the view that reality is basically matter in motion, and that all so-called non-material or mental phenomena are to be explained entirely in physical, material terms.
	[Extemporaneous, unedited formulation.]
	LP, "Founders of Western Philosophy: Thales to Hume" lecture series (1972), Lecture 2.
	[*See* **Idealism**.]
Mathematics	**Mathematics** is . . . the science of measurement, i.e., of establishing quantitative relationships.
	AR, "The Cognitive Role of Concepts," *ITOE*, 64.
Measurement	**Measurement** is the identification of a relationship— a quantitative relationship established by means of a standard that serves as a unit.
	AR, "Cognition and Measurement," *ITOE*, 7. LP discusses in "Concept-Formation as a Mathematical Process," *OPAR*, 81.
Mercy	"**Mercy**" means an unearned forgiveness.
	LP, "The Philosophy of Objectivism" lecture series (1976), Q&A Lecture 8, quoted in "Mercy," *LEX*, 290.
Metaphysical	"**Metaphysical**" [means] that which pertains to reality, to the nature of things, to existence.
	AR, "The Objectivist Ethics," *VOS*, 14.

Metaphysical Value-Judgments That aspect of metaphysics which serves as a bridge between metaphysics and ethics [is] a fundamental view of man's nature. That view involves the answers to such questions as whether the universe is knowable or not, whether man has the power of choice or not, whether he can achieve his goals in life or not. The answers to such questions are "**metaphysical value-judgments**," since they form the base of ethics.

AR, "Philosophy and Sense of Life," *RM*, 28.

Metaphysically Given The "**metaphysically given**" . . . means any fact inherent in existence apart from human action (whether mental or physical).

LP, "The Metaphysically Given as Absolute," *OPAR*, 23–24.

[*See* **Man-Made**.]

Metaphysics **Metaphysics** [is] the science that deals with the fundamental nature of reality.

AR, "The Psycho-Epistemology of Art," *RM*, 19.

Mixed Economy A **mixed economy** [is] a mixture of capitalism and statism, of freedom and controls.

AR, "The Obliteration of Capitalism," *CUI*, 185.

Money	**Money** is not merely a tool of exchange: much more importantly, it is *a tool of saving,* which permits delayed consumption and buys time for future production. To fulfill this requirement, **money** has to be some material commodity which is imperishable, rare, homogeneous, easily stored, not subject to wide fluctuations of value, and always in demand among those you trade with. AR, "Egalitarianism and Inflation," *PWNI,* 127.
Moral Perfection	**Moral perfection** is an *unbreached rationality*—not the degree of your intelligence, but the full and relentless use of your mind, not the extent of your knowledge, but the acceptance of reason as an absolute. AR, GS, *FNI,* 178–79. LP discusses in "Pride as Moral Ambitiousness," *OPAR,* 304.
Moral Values	"**Moral values**" are *chosen* values of a *fundamental* nature. LP, "Man's Life as the Standard of Moral Value," *OPAR,* 214.
Morality	A code of values accepted by choice is a code of **morality**. AR, GS, *FNI,* 122. LP discusses in "Man's Life as the Standard of Moral Value," *OPAR,* 214. [*See* **Ethics**.]

Morality, Breach of	An error of knowledge is not a moral flaw, provided you are willing to correct it. . . . But a **breach of morality** is the conscious choice of an action you know to be evil, or a willful evasion of knowledge, a suspension of sight and of thought. AR, GS, *FNI*, 179.
Music	**Music** [is the branch of art which re-creates reality by employing] the sounds produced by the *periodic* vibrations of a sonorous body, and evokes man's sense-of-life emotions. AR, "Art and Cognition," *RM*, 46.
Mysticism	**Mysticism** is the theory that man has a means of knowledge other than sense perception or reason, such as revelation, faith, intuition. LP, "Mysticism and Skepticism as Denials of Reason," *OPAR*, 182.
Nation	A "**nation**" . . . is a large number of individuals who live in the same geographical locality under the same political system. AR, "Don't Let It Go," *PWNI*, 205.
Nationalism	**Nationalism** is collectivism, with the *nation*—and in the end this means, the ethnic group or the race—as the favored collective. LP, "Some Notes about Tomorrow," *TIA*, Jul. 1992, 4.

Naturalism	**Naturalism** [in art] rejected the concept of volition and went back to a view of man as a helpless creature determined by forces beyond his control . . . [holding] that values have no power and no place, neither in human life nor in literature, that writers must present men "as they are," which meant: must record whatever they happen to see around them. AR, "The Esthetic Vacuum of Our Age," *RM*, 124. [*See* **Romanticism**.]
Nature	**Nature** is existence regarded as a system of interconnected entities governed by law; it is the universe of entities acting and interacting in accordance with their identities. LP, "Idealism and Materialism as the Rejection of Basic Axioms," *OPAR*, 31.
Necessary	"**Necessary**" names existents considered as governed by the law of identity. "To be," accordingly, *is* "to be necessary." LP, "The Metaphysically Given as Absolute," *OPAR*, 24.
Need	"**Need**" in this context denotes that which is required for survival. LP, "'Life' as the Essential Root of 'Value,'" *OPAR*, 210.

Nominalism	The essence of the theory [of **nominalism** is]: universals are merely collective names, arbitrarily imposed by men on roughly resembling particulars, by the standard of subjective human convenience. [Extemporaneous, unedited formulation.] LP, "Founders of Western Philosophy: Thales to Hume" lecture series (1972), Lecture 9.
Non-Contradiction, Law of	[The **Law of Non-Contradiction** states:] the same attribute cannot at the same time belong and not belong to the same subject and in the same respect. [Same as "Law of Contradiction."] Aristotle, *Metaphysics*, IV, 3 (W. D. Ross translation), quoted in "Contradictions," *LEX*, 107.
Novel	A **novel** is a long, fictional story about human beings and the events of their lives. AR, "Basic Principles of Literature," *RM*, 80.
Number	A "**number**" is a mental symbol that integrates units into a single larger unit (or subdivides a unit into fractions) with reference to the basic number of "one," which is the basic mental symbol of "unit." AR, "The Cognitive Role of Concepts," *ITOE*, 63.

Objective	To be "**objective**" in one's conceptual activities is volitionally to adhere to reality by following certain rules of method, a method based on facts *and* appropriate to man's form of cognition. LP, "Objectivity as Volitional Adherence to Reality by the Method of Logic," *OPAR*, 117. [*See* **Intrinsic Theory of Concepts**, **Subjective Theory of Concepts**.]
Objective Theory of the Good	The **objective theory** holds that the **good** is neither an attribute of "things in themselves" nor of man's emotional states, but *an evaluation* of the facts of reality by man's consciousness according to a rational standard of value. . . . The objective theory holds that *the good is an aspect of reality in relation to man*—and that it must be discovered, not invented, by man. AR, "What Is Capitalism?" *CUI*, 22. [*See* **Intrinsic Theory of the Good**, **Subjectivist Theory of the Good**.]
Objectivity	**Objectivity** . . . pertains to the relationship of consciousness to existence. Metaphysically, it is the recognition of the fact that reality exists independent of any perceiver's consciousness. Epistemologically, it is the recognition of the fact that a perceiver's (man's) consciousness must acquire knowledge of reality by certain means (reason) in accordance with certain rules (logic). AR, "Who Is the Final Authority in Ethics?" *VOR*, 18.

Onus of Proof	A venerable rule of logic [states] that the **onus of proof** is on him who asserts the positive, and that one must not attempt to prove a negative. LP, "The Arbitrary as Neither True Nor False," *OPAR*, 167.
"Original Sin"	[**Original sin**] means that man is evil and guilty by nature. [Invalid concept.] AR, PLB, 5.
"Package-Dealing"	[*See* **Fallacy of "Package-Dealing."**]
Painting	**Painting** [is the branch of art which re-creates reality] by means of color on a two-dimensional surface. AR, "Art and Cognition," *RM*, 46.
Perception	A "**perception**" is a group of sensations automatically retained and integrated by the brain of a living organism, which gives it the ability to be aware, not of single stimuli, but of *entities*, of things. AR, "The Objectivist Ethics," *VOS*, 20. LP discusses in "The Perceptual Level as the Given," *OPAR*, 53.
Perfection	"**Perfection**" is: flawlessly complete satisfaction of a standard of value. HB, "The Possible Dream," *TOF*, Feb. 1981, 3. [*See also* **Moral Perfection.**]

Philosophical Detection	**"Philosophical detection"** . . . is the art of discovering the fundamental premises that underlie and shape men's statements on intellectual issues. LP, "An Exercise in Philosophical Detection," *TOF*, Oct. 1981, 12.
Philosophically Objective Value	By **"philosophically objective,"** I mean a **value** estimated from the standpoint of the best possible to man, i.e., by the criterion of the most rational mind possessing the greatest knowledge, in a given category, in a given period, and in a defined context. AR, "What Is Capitalism?" *CUI*, 24. LP discusses in "Capitalism as the System of Objectivity," *OPAR*, 397. [*See* **Socially Objective Value**.]
Philosophy	**Philosophy** [is the science that] studies the *fundamental* nature of existence, of man, and of man's relationship to existence. AR, "Philosophy: Who Needs It," *PWNI*, 2.
Physical Force	**Physical force** is coercion exercised by *physical* agency, [e.g.,] by punching a man in the face, incarcerating him, shooting him, or seizing his property. LP, "The Initiation of Physical Force as Evil," *OPAR*, 310. [*See also* **Initiation of Physical Force**.]
Plot	A **plot** [in literature] is a purposeful progression of logically connected events leading to the resolution of a climax. AR, "Basic Principles of Literature," *RM*, 82. LP discusses in "Romantic Literature as Illustrating the Role of Philosophy in Art," *OPAR*, 429.

Plot-Theme	A "**plot-theme**" is the central conflict or "situation" of a story—a conflict in terms of action, corresponding to the theme and complex enough to create a purposeful progression of events. AR, "Basic Principles of Literature," *RM*, 85.
Poetry	**Poetry** is the form of literature whose medium is the sound of concepts. [Extemporaneous, unedited formulation.] LP, "Poems I Like—and Why" lecture series (1999), Lecture 1.
Political Power	The nature of **political power** [as opposed to economic power] is: the [government's] power to force obedience under threat of physical injury. . . . [It] is exercised by means of a *negative*, by the threat of punishment, injury, imprisonment, destruction. AR, "America's Persecuted Minority: Big Business," *CUI*, 46–48. There is a significant deletion in the excerpt. For a similar treatment, see LP, "Capitalism as the System of Objectivity," *OPAR*, 402. [*See* **Economic Power**.]
Politics	**Politics** [is the branch of philosophy] which defines the principles of a proper social system. AR, "Philosophy: Who Needs It," *PWNI*, 4.
Possible	A conclusion is "**possible**" if there is some, but not much, evidence in favor of it, and nothing known that contradicts it. LP, "Certainty as Contextual," *OPAR*, 176. [*See* **Certain, Probable**.]

Pride	**"Pride"** is the commitment to achieve one's own moral perfection. LP, "Pride as Moral Ambitiousness," *OPAR*, 303.
Primacy of Consciousness	The **primacy of consciousness** [is] the notion that the universe has no independent existence, that it is the product of a consciousness (either human or divine or both). AR, "The Metaphysical Versus the Man-Made," *PWNI*, 24.
Primacy of Existence	The **primacy of existence** (of reality) is the axiom that existence exists, i.e., that the universe exists independent of consciousness (of *any* consciousness), that things are what they are, that they possess a specific nature, an *identity*. AR, "The Metaphysical Versus the Man-Made," *PWNI*, 24.
Principle	A **principle** is "a fundamental, primary, or general truth, on which other truths depend." AR, "The Anatomy of Compromise," *CUI*, 144.
Probable	A conclusion is "**probable**" if the burden of a substantial body of evidence, although still inconclusive, supports it. LP, "Certainty as Contextual," *OPAR*, 178. [*See* **Certain, Possible**.]
Problem of Universals	[*See* **Universals, Problem of**.]

Production	**Production** is the application of reason to the problem of survival. AR, "What Is Capitalism?" *CUI*, 17.
Productive Work	**Productive work** is the process by which man's consciousness controls his existence, a constant process of acquiring knowledge and shaping matter to fit one's purpose, of translating an idea into physical form. AR, GS, *FNI*, 130.
Productiveness	The virtue of **productiveness** is the recognition of the fact that productive work is the process by which man's mind sustains his life. AR, "The Objectivist Ethics," *VOS*, 29.
Proof	"**Proof**" is the process of establishing truth by reducing a proposition to axioms, i.e., ultimately, to sensory evidence. LP, "Objectivity as Volitional Adherence to Reality by the Method of Logic," *OPAR*, 120.
Property, Right to	[*See* **Right to Property**.]
Psycho-Epistemology	**Psycho-epistemology** is the study of man's cognitive processes from the aspect of the interaction between the conscious mind and the automatic functions of the subconscious. AR, "The Psycho-Epistemology of Art," *RM*, 18. LP discusses in "Art as a Concretization of Metaphysics," *OPAR*, 419.

Psychologizing	**Psychologizing** consists in condemning or excusing specific individuals on the grounds of their psychological problems, real or invented, in the absence of or contrary to factual evidence. AR, "The Psychology of Psychologizing," *VOR*, 24.
Purpose	The principle of **purpose** means conscious goal-directedness in every aspect of one's existence where choice applies. LP, "Productiveness as the Adjustment of Nature to Man," *OPAR*, 298. [*See also* **Central Purpose**.]
Purposeful Action	A **purposeful action** is a conscious action caused by the agent's desire for some anticipated consequence of his action. HB, "The Analysis of Purposeful Action," *BBTC*, 34.
Racism	**Racism** is the lowest, most crudely primitive form of collectivism. It is the notion of ascribing moral, social or political significance to a man's genetic lineage—the notion that a man's intellectual and characterological traits are produced and transmitted by his internal body chemistry. AR, "Racism," *VOS*, 147; *ROP*, 179.
"Rand's Razor"	[1] Concepts are not to be multiplied beyond necessity—the corollary of which is: nor are they to be integrated in disregard of necessity. AR, "The Cognitive Role of Concepts," *ITOE*, 72. [2] **Rand's Razor** . . . states: name your primaries. LP, "Knowledge as Hierarchical," *OPAR*, 139.

Rational Self-Interest	**Rational self-interest** . . . means the ethics of selfishness, with man's life as the standard of value defining "self-interest," and rationality as the primary virtue defining the method of achieving it. LP, "The Individual as the Proper Beneficiary of His Own Moral Action," *OPAR*, 234.
Rationality	The virtue of **rationality** means the recognition and acceptance of reason as one's only source of knowledge, one's only judge of values and one's only guide to action. AR, "The Objectivist Ethics," *VOS*, 28. LP discusses in "Rationality as the Primary Virtue," *OPAR*, 221.
Rationalization	**Rationalization** is . . . a process of providing one's emotions with a false identity, of giving them spurious explanations and justifications—in order to hide one's motives, not just from others, but primarily from oneself. AR, "Philosophical Detection," *PWNI*, 18.
Reality	**Reality** is that which exists. [Axiomatic concept: not a definition.] AR, GS, *FNI*, 126.
Reason	**Reason** is the faculty that identifies and integrates the material provided by man's senses. AR, "The Objectivist Ethics," *VOS*, 22. LP discusses in Introduction to "Reason," *OPAR*, 152.

Reduction	**"Reduction"** is the process of identifying in logical sequence the intermediate steps that relate a cognitive item to perceptual data. LP, "Knowledge as Hierarchical," *OPAR*, 133.
Reification of the Zero	[*See* **Fallacy of Reification of the Zero**.]
Republic	A **"republic"** . . . is a [political] system restricted to the protection of rights. LP, "Government as an Agency to Protect Rights," *OPAR*, 368.
"Rewriting Reality"	[*See* **Fallacy of "Rewriting Reality."**]
Right	A **"right"** is a moral principle defining and sanctioning a man's freedom of action in a social context. AR, "Man's Rights," *VOS*, 110; *CUI*, 321. LP discusses in "Individual Rights as Absolutes," *OPAR*, 351.
Right of Free Speech	The **right of free speech** means that a man has the right to express his ideas without danger of suppression, interference or punitive action by the government. AR, "Man's Rights," *VOS*, 114; *CUI*, 325.
Right to Liberty	The **right to liberty** is . . . the right to think and choose, then to act in accordance with one's judgment. LP, "Individual Rights as Absolutes," *OPAR*, 352.

Right to Life	The **right to life** means the right to engage in self-sustaining and self-generated action—which means: the freedom to take all the actions required by the nature of a rational being for the support, the furtherance, the fulfillment and the enjoyment of his own life. AR, "Man's Rights," *VOS*, 110; *CUI*, 322.
Right to Property	The **right to property** is . . . the right to gain, to keep, to use and to dispose of material values. AR, "Man's Rights," *VOS*, 110–111; *CUI*, 322. LP discusses in "Individual Rights as Absolutes," *OPAR*, 352.
Right to the Pursuit of Happiness	The **right to the pursuit of happiness** is . . . the right to live for one's *own* sake and fulfillment. LP, "Individual Rights as Absolutes," *OPAR*, 352.
Romanticism	**Romanticism** is a category of art based on the recognition of the principle that man possesses the faculty of volition. AR, "What Is Romanticism?" *RM*, 99. LP discusses in "Romantic Literature as Illustrating the Role of Philosophy in Art," *OPAR*, 428. [*See* **Naturalism**.]
Rule of Fundamentality	[*See* **Fundamentality, Rule of**.]
Sacred	"**Sacred**" [means] the best, the highest possible to man. AR, "Requiem for Man," *CUI*, 303.

Sacrifice	**"Sacrifice"** is the surrender of a greater value for the sake of a lesser one or of a nonvalue.
	AR, "The Ethics of Emergencies," *VOS*, 50. LP discusses in "The Individual as the Proper Beneficiary of His Own Moral Action," *OPAR*, 232.
Sanction of the Victim	The **"sanction of the victim"** means the moral man's approval of his own martyrdom, his agreement to accept—in return for his achievements—curses, robbery, and enslavement.
	LP, "Virtue as Practical," *OPAR*, 333.
Science	**Science** is systematic knowledge gained by the use of reason based on observation.
	LP, "Idealism and Materialism as the Rejection of Basic Axioms," *OPAR*, 35.
Sculpture	**Sculpture** [is the branch of art which re-creates reality] by means of a three-dimensional form made of a solid material.
	AR, "Art and Cognition," *RM*, 46.
Self	A man's **self** is his mind—the faculty that perceives reality, forms judgments, chooses values.
	AR, "Selfishness Without a Self," *PWNI*, 50.
Self-Esteem	**Self-esteem** [is man's] inviolate certainty that his mind is competent to think and his person is worthy of happiness, which means: is worthy of living.
	AR, GS, *FNI*, 128.

Self-Evident	To be **self-evident** means to be available to direct observation, without the need of inference. HB, "Volition as Cognitive Self-Regulation" booklet, 20.
Self-Exclusion, Fallacy of	[*See* **Fallacy of Self-Exclusion**.]
Self-Generated Action	An **action** is **self-generated** when it results from the utilization of an internal energy source integral to the agent according to a directive mechanism. HB, "Self-Generation," *BBTC*, 54.
Self-Interest	[*See* **Rational Self-Interest**.]
Selfishness	The exact meaning and dictionary definition of the word "**selfishness**" is: *concern with one's own interests.* AR, Introduction, *VOS*, vii. [*See* **Egoism**.]
Sensation	A "**sensation**" is an irreducible state of awareness produced by the action of a stimulus on a sense organ. LP, "The Perceptual Level as the Given," *OPAR*, 52.
Sense of Life	A **sense of life** is a pre-conceptual equivalent of metaphysics, an emotional, subconsciously integrated appraisal of man and of existence. AR, "Philosophy and Sense of Life," *RM*, 25. LP discusses in "Art as a Concretization of Metaphysics," *OPAR*, 426.

Similarity	**Similarity**, in this context, is the relationship between two or more existents which possess the same characteristic(s), but in different measure or degree.

AR, "Concept-Formation," *ITOE*, 13. LP discusses in "Concept-Formation as a Mathematical Process," *OPAR*, 85.

Simple	The "**simple**" . . . is that which involves one, or at most a few, units.

LP, "Why Should One Act on Principle?" *TIA*, Feb. 27, 1989, 3.

[*See* **Complex**.]

Skepticism	**Skepticism** is the theory that knowledge of reality is impossible to man by any means.

LP, "Mysticism and Skepticism as Denials of Reason," *OPAR*, 183.

Social System	A **social system** is a set of moral-political-economic principles embodied in a society's laws, institutions, and government, which determine the relationships, the terms of association, among the men living in a given geographical area.

AR, "What Is Capitalism?" *CUI*, 18.

Socialism	**Socialism** [is] a theory or system of social organization which advocates the vesting of the ownership and control of the means of production, capital, land, etc., in the community as a whole.

The American College Dictionary, quoted in AR, "The New Fascism: Rule by Consensus," *CUI*, 202.

Socially Objective Value	**Socially objective value** [is] the sum of the individual judgments of all the men involved in trade at a given time, the sum of what *they* valued, each in the context of his own life. AR, "What Is Capitalism?" *CUI*, 24–25. LP discusses in "Capitalism as the System of Objectivity," *OPAR*, 398. [Same as "market value."] [*See* **Philosophically Objective Value**.]
Society	**Society** is a large number of men who live together in the same country, and who deal with one another. AR, "Textbook of Americanism," *ARC*, 88.
Soul	**Soul** [means] the essence of a person, which is his mind and its basic values. LP, "Reason as an Attribute of the Individual," *OPAR*, 202.
Spiral Theory of Knowledge	The **spiral theory** [**of knowledge**] is simply this idea: first we learn a given idea; then we leave it—we move to something else, we learn other subjects. Then we encounter the original idea again, but now with more knowledge, with a deeper context. [Extemporaneous, unedited formulation.] LP, "Understanding Objectivism" lecture series (1984), Lecture 3.
Spiritual	By "**spiritual**" I mean "pertaining to consciousness." AR, "Concepts of Consciousness," *ITOE*, 33.

Standard	A "**standard**" is an abstract principle that serves as a measurement or gauge to guide a man's choices in the achievement of a concrete, specific purpose. AR, "The Objectivist Ethics," *VOS*, 27. LP discusses in "The Individual as the Proper Beneficiary of His Own Moral Action," *OPAR*, 229.
Standard of Value	The **standard of value** of the Objectivist ethics—the standard by which one judges what is good or evil—is *man's life*, or: that which is required for man's survival *qua* man. Since reason is man's basic means of survival, that which is proper to the life of a rational being is the good; that which negates, opposes or destroys it is the evil. AR, "The Objectivist Ethics," *VOS*, 25. LP discusses issue in "Man's Life as the Standard of Moral Value," *OPAR*, 219. [*See* **Man's Survival qua Man**.]
Statism	"**Statism**" means any system that concentrates power in the state at the expense of individual freedom. LP, "Statism as the Politics of Unreason," *OPAR*, 369.
"Stolen Concept"	[*See* **Fallacy of the "Stolen Concept."**]
Study	**Study** is persistent, careful, concentrated effort to acquire and retain a body of knowledge. HB, "How to Study Ayn Rand's Writings" lecture (1994).

Style	"**Style**" is a particular, distinctive or characteristic mode of execution. AR, "Art and Sense of Life," *RM*, 40.
Stylized	"**Stylized**" means condensed to essential characteristics, which are chosen according to an artist's view of man. AR, "Art and Cognition," *RM*, 67.
Subjective	The **subjective** means the arbitrary, the irrational, the blindly emotional. AR, "Art and Moral Treason," *RM*, 150. [*See* **Objective**.]
Subjective Theory of Concepts	[Certain] schools [of thought] regard **concepts** as **subjective**, i.e., as products of man's consciousness, unrelated to the facts of reality, as mere "names" or notions arbitrarily assigned to arbitrary groupings of concretes on the ground of vague, inexplicable resemblances. AR, "Definitions," *ITOE*, 53. [*See* **Intrinsic Theory of Concepts**.] [*See also* **Objective**.]
Subjectivism	**Subjectivism** is the belief that reality is not a firm absolute, but a fluid, plastic, indeterminate realm which can be altered, in whole or in part, by the consciousness of the perceiver—i.e., by his feelings, wishes or whims. AR, "Who Is the Final Authority in Ethics?" *VOR*, 19. [*See* **Objectivity**.]

Subjectivist Theory of the Good	The **subjectivist theory** holds that the **good** bears no relation to the facts of reality, that it is the product of a man's consciousness, created by his feelings, desires, "intuitions," or whims, and that it is merely an "arbitrary postulate" or an "emotional commitment." AR, "What Is Capitalism?" *CUI*, 21–22. [*See* **Intrinsic Theory of the Good**, **Objective Theory of the Good**.]
Supernaturalism	**Supernaturalism** [is] the view that reality is a higher, spiritual dimension (like God and Heaven), in relation to which this world is low and unreal. LP, "The 'Mystery' of Heaven's Gate," *TIA*, Jul. 1997, 3.
Theme	A **theme** [in literature] is the summation of a novel's abstract meaning. AR, "Basic Principles of Literature," *RM*, 81.
Theory	A **theory** . . . is a set of abstract principles purporting to be either a correct description of reality or a set of guidelines for man's actions. AR, "Philosophical Detection," *PWNI*, 14.
Thinking	All **thinking** is a process of identification and integration. AR, GS, *FNI*, 125.
Time	**Time** is measurement of motion; as such, it is a type of relationship. LP, "The Philosophy of Objectivism" lecture series (1976), Q&A Lecture 2, quoted in "Time," *LEX*, 503.

Trade	"**Trade**" ... denotes a voluntary exchange of values.
	LP, "Capitalism as the Only Moral Social System," *OPAR*, 386.

Trader	A **trader** is a man who earns what he gets and does not give or take the undeserved.
	AR, GS, *FNI*, 133. LP discusses in "Justice as Rationality in the Evaluation of Men," *OPAR*, 286–287.

Truth	**Truth** is the recognition of reality.
	AR, GS, *FNI*, 126. LP discusses in "The Arbitrary as Neither True Nor False," *OPAR*, 165.

Tyranny	**Tyranny** is any political system (whether absolute monarchy or fascism or communism) that does not recognize individual rights (which necessarily include property rights).
	AR, "From a Symposium," *ROP*, 173.

Ultimate Value	An **ultimate value** is that final goal or end to which all lesser goals are the means—and it sets the standard by which all lesser goals are *evaluated*.
	AR, "The Objectivist Ethics," *VOS*, 17. LP discusses issue in "'Life' as the Essential Root of 'Value,'" *OPAR*, 212.

Understand	To **understand** means to focus on the content of a given subject ... to isolate its essentials, to establish its relationship to the previously known, and to integrate it with the appropriate categories of other subjects. Integration is the essential part of understanding.
	AR, "The Comprachicos," *ROP*, 68.

Unit	A **unit** is an existent regarded as a separate member of a group of two or more similar members. AR, "Cognition and Measurement," *ITOE*, 6. LP discusses in "Differentiation and Integration as the Means to a Unit-Perspective," *OPAR*, 75.

Unit-Economy	The essence . . . of man's incomparable cognitive power is the ability to reduce a vast amount of information to a minimal number of units—which is the task performed by his conceptual faculty. [The essence is the ability to **economize the units** required to hold in mind a given content.] AR, "The Cognitive Role of Concepts," *ITOE*, 63. Material in brackets was provided by LP for this glossary. It is an extemporaneous, unedited formulation by LP, adapted from LP, "Concepts as Devices to Achieve Unit-Economy," *OPAR*, 106. [*See* **"Crow Epistemology."**]

Universals, Problem of	[Defenders of conceptual knowledge] were unable to offer a solution to the "**problem of universals**," that is: to define the nature and source of abstractions, to determine the relationship of concepts to perceptual data—and to prove the validity of scientific induction. AR, "For the New Intellectual," *FNI*, 30.

Universe	The **universe** is the total of that which exists. LP, "The Philosophy of Objectivism" lecture series (1976), Lecture 2, quoted in "Universe," *LEX*, 517.

Utilitarianism	**Utilitarianism** . . . holds that man's duty is to serve . . . "the greatest happiness of the greatest number." LP, "Kant Versus America," *OP*, 119.

Validation	**"Validation"** . . . subsumes any process of establishing an idea's relationship to reality, whether deductive reasoning, inductive reasoning, or perceptual self-evidence. LP, "Existence, Consciousness, and Identity as the Basic Axioms," *OPAR*, 8.
Value	**"Value"** is that which one acts to gain and/or keep. AR, "The Objectivist Ethics," *VOS*, 16, 27. LP discusses in "'Life' as the Essential Root of 'Value,'" *OPAR*, 208. [*See also* **Moral Values, Ultimate Value**.]
Violence	**"Violence"** names . . . force that is swift, intense, rough, and/or accompanied by fury. LP, "The Initiation of Physical Force as Evil," *OPAR*, 319.
Virtue	**"Virtue"** is the action by which one gains and keeps [a value]. AR, GS, *FNI*, 121. LP discusses in "Rationality as the Primary Virtue," *OPAR*, 221.
Volition	Man's **volition** is an attribute of his consciousness (of his rational faculty) and consists in the choice to perceive existence or to evade it. [Axiomatic concept: not a definition.] AR, "The Metaphysical Versus the Man-Made," *PWNI*, 25. [Same as "free will." *See* **Free Will**.]

Whim	A "**whim**" is a desire experienced by a person who does not know and does not care to discover its cause. AR, "The Objectivist Ethics," *VOS*, 14. LP discusses in "Rationality as the Primary Virtue," *OPAR*, 228.
Word	A **word** is merely a visual-auditory symbol used to represent a concept. AR, "Definitions," *ITOE*, 40.
Zero, Reification of the	[*See* **Fallacy of Reification of the Zero.**]

About the Editors

Allison T. Kunze majored in Philosophy at Randolph-Macon Woman's College (Lynchburg, Virginia), graduating Phi Beta Kappa in 1975. In the early 1980s, she compiled her own (unpublished) dictionary of terms defined by Ayn Rand. She later aided Harry Binswanger in the preparation of *The Ayn Rand Lexicon: Objectivism from A to Z*, by cross-checking her dictionary against his manuscript, to identify additional entries for inclusion in the *Lexicon*. A Montessori teacher for over twenty-five years, she is currently retired and lives with her husband in Columbus, Ohio, near their wonderful children and grandchildren.

Jean F. Moroney received a BS and MS in Electrical Engineering from MIT. After leaving engineering in 1992 to pursue a career in psycho-epistemology, she received an MS in Psychology from Carnegie Mellon in 1994, and a graduation certificate from the Objectivist Graduate Center of the Ayn Rand Institute in 1996. She now runs a business called Thinking Directions, offering individual and corporate programs on the mental side of productivity. She lives in Naples, Florida, with her husband, Harry Binswanger.

AYN RAND'S NOVELS

We the Living (1936): Set in Soviet Russia, this is Ayn Rand's first and most autobiographical novel. Its theme: "the individual against the state, the supreme value of a human life and the evil of the totalitarian state that claims the right to sacrifice it."

Anthem (1938): This novelette depicts a world of the future, a society so collectivized that even the word "I" has vanished from the language. *Anthem*'s theme: the meaning and glory of man's ego.

The Fountainhead (1943): The story of an innovator—architect Howard Roark—and his battle against a tradition-worshiping society. Its theme: "individualism versus collectivism, not in politics, but in man's soul; the psychological motivations and the basic premises that produce the character of an individualist or a collectivist." This was Ayn Rand's first projection of the ideal man.

Atlas Shrugged (1957): Ayn Rand's complete philosophy, dramatized in the form of a mystery story "not about the murder of a man's body, but about the murder—and rebirth—of man's spirit." The story is set in a near-future United States whose economy is collapsing due to the inexplicable disappearance of the country's leading innovators and industrialists—the "Atlases" on whom the world rests. The theme: "the role of the mind in man's existence—and, as corollary, the demonstration of a new moral philosophy: the morality of rational self-interest."

AYN RAND'S OTHER FICTION

Night of January 16th (1934): A courtroom play in which the verdict depends on the sense of life of jurors selected from the audience.

The Early Ayn Rand (1984): A collection of stories and plays written by Ayn Rand in the 1920s and 1930s, plus passages cut from *The Fountainhead*.

AYN RAND'S NONFICTION

For the New Intellectual (1961): A collection of the key philosophical passages from her novels. The forty-eight-page title essay sweeps over the history of thought, showing how ideas control the course of history and how philosophy has served for the most part as an engine of destruction.

The Virtue of Selfishness (1964): Ayn Rand presents her revolutionary concept of egoism in essays on the morality of rational selfishness and the political implications of her moral philosophy. Essays include: "The Objectivist Ethics," "Man's Rights," "The Nature of Government" and "Racism."

Capitalism: The Unknown Ideal (1966): Essays on the theory and history of capitalism demonstrating it as the only moral economic system, i.e., the only one consistent with individual rights and a free society. Includes: "What Is Capitalism?," "The Roots of War," "Conservatism: An Obituary" and "The Anatomy of Compromise."

Introduction to Objectivist Epistemology (1967): The Objectivist theory of concepts and Ayn Rand's solution to "the problem of universals," identifying the relationship of abstractions to concretes. Includes an essay by Leonard Peikoff, "The Analytic-Synthetic Dichotomy." The second edition (1990) includes transcripts of Ayn Rand's workshops on her theory—containing her answers to questions raised by philosophers and other academics.

The Romantic Manifesto (1969): Ayn Rand's philosophy of art, with a new analysis of the Romantic school of literature. Essays include: "Philosophy and Sense of Life" and "What Is Romanticism?"

Philosophy: Who Needs It (1982): This book demonstrates that philosophy is essential in each person's life. Essays include: "Philosophical Detection," "Causality Versus Duty" and "The Metaphysical Versus the Man-Made."

The Ayn Rand Lexicon: Objectivism from A to Z (1986): A mini-encyclopedia of Objectivism, containing the key passages from the writings of Ayn Rand and her associates on 400 topics in philosophy and related fields. Edited by Harry Binswanger.

The Voice of Reason: Essays in Objectivist Thought (1989): Philosophy and cultural analysis, including "Who Is the Final Authority in Ethics?" Also "Religion Versus America" by Leonard Peikoff and "Libertarianism: The Perversion of Liberty" by Peter Schwartz.

The Ayn Rand Column (1991): Ayn Rand's columns for the *Los Angeles Times*, and other essays.

Ayn Rand's Marginalia (1995): Notes Ayn Rand made in the margins of the works of more than twenty authors, including Barry Goldwater, C. S. Lewis and Ludwig von Mises. Edited by Robert Mayhew.

Letters of Ayn Rand (1995): This collection of more than 500 letters offers much new information on Ayn Rand's life as a philosopher, novelist, political activist and Hollywood screenwriter. Edited by Michael S. Berliner.

Journals of Ayn Rand (1997): An extensive collection of Ayn Rand's thoughts—spanning forty years—on literature and philosophy, including notes on her major novels and on the development of the political philosophy of individualism. Edited by David Harriman.

The Ayn Rand Reader (1998): This collection combines extensive excerpts from all of Ayn Rand's novels as well as her nonfiction work. Recommended for readers new to Ayn Rand and for those already familiar with her work. Edited by Gary Hull and Leonard Peikoff.

Return of the Primitive: The Anti-Industrial Revolution (1999) [formerly *The New Left: The Anti-Industrial Revolution* (1971)]: Ayn Rand's answer to environmentalism, "progressive" education and other contemporary anti-reason movements, with additional essays by editor Peter Schwartz.

The Art of Fiction (1999): Based on Ayn Rand's 1958 course on the unity of the four essential elements of fiction: theme, plot, characterization and style. Edited by Tore Boeckman.

The Art of Nonfiction: A Guide for Writers and Readers (2001): From the edited transcripts of Ayn Rand's 1969 private nonfiction writing course. Edited by Robert Mayhew; Introduction by Peter Schwartz.

For further information about Objectivism, and the most complete selection of Ayn Rand's writings and lectures available—please contact the Ayn Rand Institute:

The Ayn Rand Institute
6 Hutton Centre Drive
Suite 600
Santa Ana, CA 92707

TELEPHONE:
1-949-222-6550

aynrand.org

www.ingramcontent.com/pod-product-compliance
Lightning Source LLC
Chambersburg PA
CBHW050604280326
41933CB00011B/1977